EDINBURGH TRAMWAYS ALBUM

D. L. G. HUNTER, C.Eng.

TURNTABLE PUBLICATIONS
SHEFFIELD

40p

FIRST PUBLISHED 1972
Reprinted 1974

All unacknowledged photographs from Author's collection.

BY THE SAME AUTHOR

Edinburgh's Transport
Carriages and Wagons of the Highland Railway
Scottish Electric Tramways
Scottish Buses Before 1928

ISBN 0 902844 09 1

Cover Photo: Courtesy of F. C. Inglis & Son Ltd

Printed by Crown Press (Keighley) Limited, Chapel Lane, Keighley

AN EDINBURGH TRAMWAYS ALBUM

INTRODUCTION

Following the passing of the Tramways Act of 1870 tracks were laid in many cities and towns, services by horse-drawn tramcars commencing during the following few years.

In Edinburgh and Leith — then a separate burgh — tracks were laid by the Edinburgh Street Tramways Co., and the first route, from Bernard St. in Leith up Leith Walk to Edinburgh and along Princes St. to Haymarket opened on 6th November 1871.

Considerable extensions were made in all directions, but on 9th December 1893 Edinburgh Corporation, having decided to install a system of cable traction, exercised their right to acquire the system within the city boundaries, and lease it to the Edinburgh and District Tramways Co. Limited, who through their parent company, Dick Kerr & Co. Limited, were to build the cable system. The route to Portobello however remained in the hands of the E.S.T. Co. Limited for a few years more until the city having absorbed Portobello, the final length of the route changed hands on 30th June 1898. Kitson steam engines had hauled some of the cars on this route in 1881-2.

Meanwhile, the Edinburgh Northern Tramways Co. had built and opened a cable line from Hanover St. to Goldenacre on 28th January 1888, followed by another line from Frederick St. to Comely Bank. This system passed to the Corporation, and the Edinburgh & District Tramways Co. Limited on 1st July 1897. The first reconstructed horse-car route from the Leith boundary at Pilrig and along Princes St. to Tollcross and Morningside and beyond to a new terminus at Braid Hills Rd. was opened to cable cars on 26th October 1899. Subsequently, nearly all the horse-car routes in the City were converted to cable operation and there were several extensions and some new routes as well.

At this period the Edinburgh Street Tramways Co. continued to operate the remainder of their system situated in the burgh of Leith and also built some extensions to it — all still operated by horse-drawn cars, but on 23rd October 1904, Leith Corporation bought over the E.S.T.Co. system and forthwith electrified it on the overhead system. The first electric cars of Leith Corporation ran from the foot of Leith Walk via Pilrig to Stanley Rd. on 18th August 1905. The extension round the Granton circle followed in 1909. The last horse-cars to run in Edinburgh operated from Tollcross via Gilmore Place to Colinton Rd., and these ceased on 24th August 1907.

The Musselburgh Electric Tramways had opened their electric line from Levenhall through Musselburgh and over the Edinburgh boundary to meet the Edinburgh cars at the Joppa terminus on 12th December 1904. This company extended their line from Levenhall to Port Seton in 1909.

Edinburgh Corporation also built a short electric line from Ardmillan Terrace to Slateford which was opened by the E.&D.T. Co. Limited on 8th June 1910.

The E.&D.T. Co.'s lease expired on 30th June 1919, and Edinburgh Corporation then took over the cable system and converted it — with minor exceptions — to electric operation. The Burgh of Leith was incorporated within the City from November 1920, so that the first electric cars in the centre of Edinburgh on 20th June 1922, ran from the various Leith termini up Leith Street and the Bridges to Nether Liberton and Churchill via the Grange. Princes Street itself was converted in a commendable overnight operation on 21st/22nd October 1922. Conversion of the other routes and considerable extensions followed, and when cable cars finally ceased to operate on 23rd June 1923, with the conversion of Portobello route, through running with the Musselburgh and District Electric Light and Traction Co.'s system to Port Seton was also inaugurated. The latter Company, however, gave up tramway operation in 1928, and thereafter Edinburgh Corporation Cars terminated at Levenhall. The route between Joppa and Levenhall was subsequently purchased by Edinburgh Corporation and rebuilt to their standards.

The last extension to the Edinburgh system to be opened was from North Gyle farm to the Maybury on 14th February 1937. Subsequently, an extension along Ferry Road to Crewe Toll was partly constructed but with the advent of war in 1939 it was never completed.

The Corporation took the first steps towards closing down the system when the Comely Bank route was replaced by buses on 1st June 1952. Other route closures followed steadily until in October 1956 electric cars were running only from Granton Rd. Stn. and from the foot of Craighall Rd., the former via Hanover Street and the latter via Pilrig Street, York Place and Princes Street to the Mound where they combined to proceed via the Mound and Tollcross to the Braids.

These routes were closed with due ceremony on 16th November 1956, so ending eighty-five years of tramway operation in Edinburgh.

If you have found this small book interesting and would like to know more about Edinburgh's trams — and buses etc. — you will find a fully detailed history in "Edinburgh's Transport" by the same author, published by the Advertiser Press Ltd., Huddersfield, by whose kind permission several of these illustrations are reproduced.

A horse car of the Edinburgh Street Tramways Company with "knife-board" roof seat, probably in the eighteen-eighties. (Anon.)

An early type of horse car rebuilt with "garden" seats and as running about 1900. (Block Courtesy of E.C.T.)

Edinburgh & District Tramways Company horse car No. 72 at the Tollcross terminus of the Colinton Road route just before closure in 1907. Some of the last horse cars were rebuilt as cable cars and three eventually became electric cars, viz.: Nos. 15, 17 and 19. (Anon.)

Edinburgh Northern Tramways Company's cable car for the Trinity route: E.&D.T. Co. Nos. 121-8.

(Block Courtesy Advertiser Press Ltd.)

Edinburgh Northern Tramways Company's cable car for the Stockbridge route: E.&D.T.Co. Nos. 129-136. (Anon.)

Edinburgh Northern Tramways Company's improved cable car: E.&D.T. Co. Nos. 139-144. (Anon.)

Leith Corporation open-top car, Brush built type, on trial run.
(Block Courtesy Advertiser Press Ltd.)

Leith Corporation closed-top car, B.T.H. built type. (Anon.)

Leith Corporation's watering car.

Musselburgh Electric Tramways open-top car. (Anon.)

Edinburgh & District Tramway Company standard cable car of 1899, No. 208, one of one hundred and twenty built by Brown Marshall & Company; photographed about 1919 with City crest. Twenty-five similar cars were also built by G. F. Milnes & Company in 1899-1900.

E.&D.T.Co. cable car converted for Slateford electric route in 1910: these were Nos. 28, 38, 64 and 74.

(Block Courtesy Advertiser Press Ltd.)

Many standard cable cars were fitted with top covers between 1907-12: This view of No. 46, one of those built by G. F. Milnes & Company, is about 1921. (F.C.I.)

In 1920 Edinburgh Corporation fitted new improved top covers to many cable cars.

By 1922 some had platform vestibules too: This is No. 33.
(Block Courtesy Advertiser Press Ltd.)

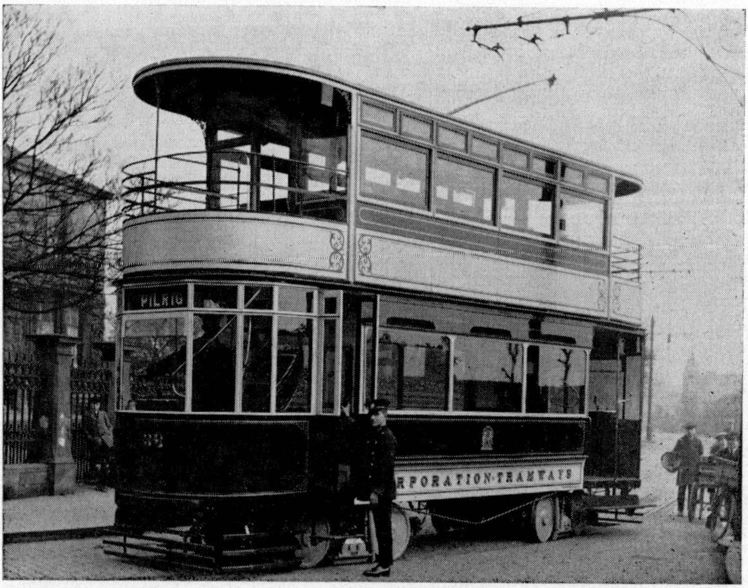

One of the first cable cars converted for electric traction was tried for a short time on bogies and ran thus on the Leith system.
(Block Courtesy Advertiser Press Ltd.)

From October 1899 to June 1922 passengers between Edinburgh and Leith had to change cars at the boundary at Pilrig. A view taken about 1906. (Block Courtesy Advertiser Press Ltd.)

The scene at Pilrig on 20th June 1922. A large crowd cheers the first electric car on to the newly electrified track up to the Post Office and Nether Liberton. (E.O.C.)

For the next four months a few cable cars still ran to Pilrig and electric and cable cars could be seen on the same track.
(Block Courtesy Advertiser Press Ltd.)

Some of the cable cars were converted to open-top electric cars. This view shows one of the first cars using the temporary track in Princes Street on the morning of 22nd October 1922, following the overnight conversion of Princes Street.

(Block Courtesy Advertiser Press Ltd.)

Twenty cable cars Nos. 209-228 were built by Dick Kerr & Company in 1903 and fitted with top-covers in 1907. Shortly after this view at Joppa cable traction ceased. A Musselburgh single-deck electric car is seen in the background.

(Block Courtesy Advertiser Press Ltd.)

Musselburgh closed-top car on through service from Edinburgh G.P.O. to Port Seton at Joppa. The car in the background is a cable car as converted to electric traction. (E.O.C.)

An early and lone example of an all-enclosed car was No. 222, a converted cable car of Dick Kerr type in which the 1907 top-cover was used. It was nick-named the "Crystal Palace".

A few of the old Northern Company's cable cars also became electric cars: Nos. 76, 86 and 112 were similar to this one.

These, and certain others, later became salt spreading/snow plough cars. No. 86 shown here had six windows.

The Dick Kerr built cable cars were among the last to be converted to electric cars with new top-covers: They were fitted with air-operated track brakes and used on the Mound, Hanover Street and Comely Bank routes.

One of the new electric cars built for Edinburgh Corporation. The Peckham P22 truck was standard until the thirties.
(Block Courtesy Advertiser Press Ltd.)

These cars later had the top deck verandahs enclosed and transverse seats provided in the lower saloon.

The Dick Kerr converted cable cars and some similar cars built by the E.&D.T.Co. at Shrubhill 1905-11 were the last to be thus modernised in 1931-3. Four of the latter had a slightly raised lower saloon floor, the step to which can be seen. These four were Nos. 54, 59, 66 and 72. The headlight was fitted during the war.
(Block Courtesy Advertiser Press Ltd.)

The former Leith Corporation closed-top cars were rebuilt with platform vestibules and lengthened wheelbase in 1924-5.

Some of them were put on standard Peckham trucks in 1932.

This was the first of a series of all-enclosed cars built at Shrubhill 1929-31. The livery shown was not perpetuated.

Another of these cars in the normal colour scheme of the period, seen at the West End.

Ten similar cars were built by R. Y. Pickering & Company in 1932 and had M.&T. trucks. They were provided with headlights, a fitting not hitherto used though most of the former Leith Corporation cars retained theirs.

The experimental straight-sided car No. 180 which appeared in 1932 created quite a stir and was painted bright red. It had an E.M.B. truck at first as shown, and later an M.&T. truck.
(Block Courtesy Advertiser Press Ltd.)

The first pair of cars of all-metal construction came from Metropolitan-Cammel also in 1932. They were Nos. 260 and 265 and also had M.&T. trucks.

No. 261 was another "one-off" car of composite construction built at Shrubhill.

The Portobello route was the scene of a trial of a pantograph on No. 73 in 1933. A bow collector had similarly been tried in 1925. The adoption of carbon-insert trolley heads in 1940 was the ultimate answer to current collection problems. Note also the less elaborate lining and lettering adopted at this time.

Six more all-metal cars came from Metropolitan-Cammel in 1934: These were of much improved appearance and were fitted with turntable type seats. Only this one No. 249 had the doors on the platform. The others were Nos. 241-2/4-6. All had M.&T. trucks.

(Block Courtesy Advertiser Press Ltd.)

Hurst Nelson & Company built three similar cars Nos. 231/8-9, also on M.&T. trucks.

The first three all-metal "streamline" shape cars came from the English Electric Company in 1934: They were Nos. 262-3/7. No. 12 shown here is one of twenty similar cars Nos. 11-30 of 1935: This one was built by Hurst, Nelson & Company. Some had M.&T. trucks. (Block Courtesy Advertiser Press Ltd.)

A new standard type of car of composite construction was built at Shrubhill in 1934: These used the standard Peckham P22 truck. Eighty-four were eventually built, the last in 1950.
(Block Courtesy Advertiser Press Ltd.)

Decorated cars appeared on special occasions such as the Floral car for a Royal visit in July 1934. It was No. 50.
(Block Courtesy of E.C.T.)

No. 58 fresh from the paint shop during the war with white fenders, masked headlight and anti-blast netting on the lower saloon windows.

Eleven cars were bought second-hand from Manchester Corporation after the war and used on the Levenhall route. They were Nos. 401-11. Numbers 372-400 were never used.

One of the older cars in the post-war livery.

The upper saloon of a Leith Corporation car: No. 247.

The lower saloon of a converted cable car: No. 9.
(Block Courtesy Advertiser Press Ltd.)

The upper saloon of a Shrubhill 1934 standard car: No. 220.
(Block Courtesy Advertiser Press Ltd.)

The lower saloon of a Shrubhill 1934 standard car: No. 218.
(Block Courtesy Advertiser Press Ltd.)

The last week: Even the rail grinder made a journey.

A standard car enters Princes Street from St Andrew Street.

The illuminated car which toured the system during the last week: It was No. 172.

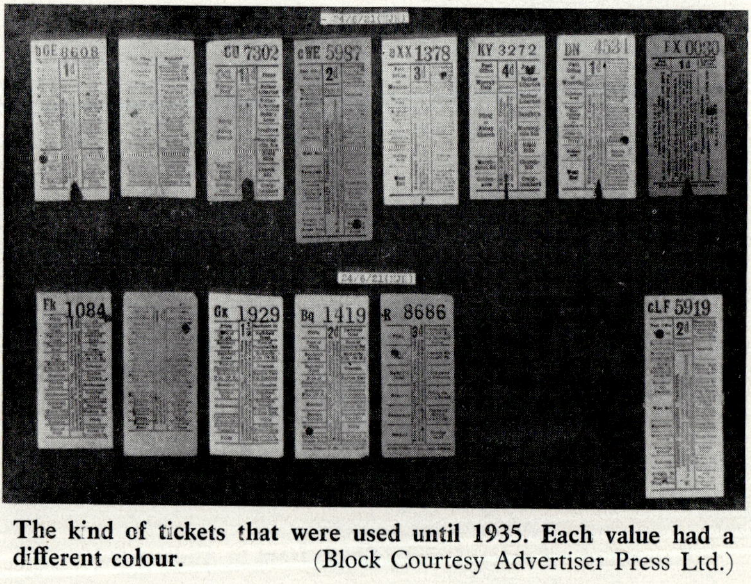

The kind of tickets that were used until 1935. Each value had a different colour. (Block Courtesy Advertiser Press Ltd.)